I0836802

SPECTRAL FOREST

Nisha Bhakoo

Published in Dundee by **The Onslaught Press**
19 A Corso Street, DD2 1DR
31 October 2020

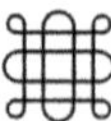

The cover image is a reworking of a **Philippe Saltel** etching
from the 2010 artists' book *Poison Trees*
republished in 2014 by the Onslaught Press

ISBN: **978-1-912111-86-2**

The title on the front cover and title page is set in James Grieshaber's ***trattatello***.

For Michael

Argan

The fleshy fruit of my body
is tender. Jolted
by the dehydrated roads
of Essaouira.
I lick the strawberry laces
in a wilting hand.
Distraction, in sugar.
I find it also on the other side
of the bus's splintered window—
Goats perched on branches
one-two-three-four-five—
the stoic tree blurs
out of eyesight.
Even wild bees seek its time.
The fatty liquid
in the cracked nuts
of this crooked tree,
is adored worldwide.
It bewitches saucepans,
soothes hungry mouths.
Eases tough locks
in oily lullaby.
How does the Argan tree
keep its ego in check,
when its slender branches
drip in goats and gold?

Forest bathing (1)

A flurry of rain
on the island that glows green
with Yakusugi.

Thick winter coat

I took the rain home from the forest.
And in exchange,

I laid down the beehive of mind.
Glittering droplets on my thick winter coat:

a reminder that a moment is not lost,
it can be carried home through the heart.

The forest was a portal to the divine.
The deep silence, a reminder of

the hand that guides the breeze,
the glue that holds the thrashing ocean together.

Under the moonlight, I surrendered.
I laid down venomous thoughts,

to taste the weather on my tongue,
to open my eyes to the intricate patterns of bark:

a reminder that we do not live in chaos.
The divine can be seen in the simplest of things:

the turning of the seasons,
the tiny gemstones of rain.

Cinematic

I am froth. I am fantasy.
I am tracking your heart. I am sleeping in bleaching darkness.
I am both drinker and drunk on expansion.
I am chewing ginger.
I am caramelising fear.
I am unmarried. I am a rare touch.
I am looking into your eyes you give nothing away.
I am sex. I am deserving.
I am faraway eyes. I am spitting fire.
I am difference.
I am dark water.
I am an island of old wounds.
I am evasive. I am careful when choosing friends.
I am living many lives in one.
I am living life like this is my only one.
I am inclined to give the fruit of my lessons away:

treat
life
like
it
is
cinema.

KINO

Griebnitzsee

we didn't check the weather / inky June mood
an overlooked element / at Griebnitzsee
a piercing drop of temperature / arm hairs know it
biergarten / droplets on tiny knuckles
serviettes beer-soaked /

i didn't want to ask for new ones /
my accent makes a fuss /
i have lived in Germany for five years /
& my name is still foreign /
in every country i have lived /
i am a stranger to myself /

the sky is smouldering

you have felt belonging / i wonder how it feels
different sensitivities to the environment /
you laugh at my descriptions of Brandenburg /
a kind teasing / at the curve of my imagination /
my stereotypes of fairy tale forests

we think in different languages / after all
you are attracted to capitalist success /
I am revolted by capitalist "success" /

now i have made peace with the inadequacies of speech /
my experience / i have to write it for myself /
i don't know another way of living / of traversing foreign landscapes /

the heavens open

to another table / frantic / throwing our damp bodies into dry seats
protected by a canopy of beech / we breathe in a cushioned relief /
watching fat pearls of rain explode /
i feel safe here

Forest bathing (2)

The snowmelt rivers
from Mount Ontake in the West
are lonesome tonight.

An un-special day

I will remember—
frost on your eyelashes.
I will remember—
the calling of the crow
as we entered the forest,
we wanted to lose
the heaviness of our bones,
surrendering ourselves
to pine trees.
To try on new bodies
in movement without purpose.
I will remember—
tiny drops of condensation
on our flask of Earl Grey
and the salty crisps
we ate in a hurry
in the chirping of
an overcast morning.
An un-special day,
examining pinecones,
made special by escape.

Floating

a water lily /
enlivens cloudy water//
a tiny heart swells /

Sweet Chestnut

Sweet Chestnut tried to tame me.
Chided me, when I came in the darkest rain,
stayed home when others frolicked in light.
Sometimes I'd chat incessantly,
to be torn by a stab of its silence.
In Spring, it would punish me
by throwing down hard fruit.
I didn't understand how its blade-like leaves
could wave around victoriously
in those ruined moments.

But there were times, I felt at peace,
gazing up at its grey-purple, protective body.
Sweet Chestnut, dutifully dimmed its sharp eyes
and let me run my fingers along
spears of pale-yellow flowers.
Sometimes I was given a translucent leaf
to closely admire,
a gift of unspoken intimacy.
I saw under Sweet Chestnut's prickly casing,
and returned when the rain whistled at my window,
at the approach of another eccentric evening.

tourist in dresden

no blood for the soil / this month
desires of security / can wait

dresden skyline / wrong time of month
to be a tourist / rubbing tiger balm

on crying feet / at a man's heels
can't stop menstruating / konzert in der Frauenkirche

greasy fingertips / made for witchery
next month / double blood

for wounded soil / I weep
matters of creation / deconstruction

the city waits patiently /
to rebuild

The Shadow of the Mersey*

History will haunt
until it is acknowledged.
A slosh of settled attitude
enveloped a body,
the heart was a river run dry
of blood.
Charles Wooton fled 18 Upper Pitt Street,
Liverpool?
A question rather than a bed,
always on the look-out—
eyes in the back of the head.
But what good is it when eyes can alert
then do nothing but blink?
He ran for his life
before three hundred pairs of
narrowed eyes and
through the tightest teeth—
the scariest soundbites of
fractured white masculinity.
Their butch stones brought him
to the base of the Mersey,
his body birthing a new fear every time
it was hit,
until all fears were released.
His twenty-four years eclipsed by tragic end,
he was much more
than this one event—
Charles Wootton
he splashed around like a fish out of water
except he was in water—
drowning.

History will repeat
until it is acknowledged.
Pain will resurface
until it is felt.
I spent my teenage years,
looking across the Mersey river
to an imposing city I didn't know was built
on the slave trade.
The ebb and flow of the brown water
at Hamilton Square,
made me feel nauseous
I couldn't locate the why.
Colonialism didn't make it into
the textbooks in my high-school classroom.
I didn't know Charles Wootton's story,
until I was in my thirties.
Long after I had left Merseyside.
History will haunt.
History will haunt.
History will haunt.
Until it is acknowledged.

*Inspired by the story of Charles Wootton, born in Bermuda. This black man was killed by a white mob in Liverpool—he was chased into the River Mersey and pelted with stones until he drowned on 5 June 1919.

Spectral Forest

the razor-sharp eyes of machinery / can't see:

what is lost what is lost

indigenous ground hacked into meat /

poisoning the heartbeats yet to form /

the world's greatest forest has PTSD /

the throat of the soil /

spluttering up blood coins /

mass destruction in Amazonia /

small-print in our weekly newspaper /

what is lost what is lost

will haunt will revenge

Tender Island

The city of London was sweltering. Out of breath to the hotel door,
switch on estrangement (click). A city that can put your name in lights
(if you can plot in the dark). You don't have to wear clothes in the dark—
but there is nothing tender about this room, but this isn't a tender island.
A single dog sings his soul in a city that I'm not part of . . . anymore.
But the TV gives a hand to hold, in this awkward hour,
a documentary on Fleetwood Mac takes me to someone else's childhood.
Being alone isn't loneliness (until you fall in love). The night opens up—

But my hair smells of the day. The big smoke told me to *keep moving*.
The night is a dash (click). I trust myself to know how to sleep.
I'd rather be here than on a midnight flight.
So—I will let my hair tangle into a nest as I sleep,
the little insect crawling on my thumb can bite off what it needs.
Will England see my dreams on a TV screen?
I envy the bed of yesterday and tomorrow. I lived on this island once.
At 34, I'm still afraid of silence. And this island is built on blood-stained silence.

TV Producer

If you scrunch your eyes to the point of blood, you will become a television screen. You will see yourself within four walls. Vomiting light. Sleeping in colour. Kicking against a trapdoor.

I know what came before your eyes.
It was the size of a passport. It was the weight of stamp.

It was a star of a man, unknown and dull. He was not shining, but he understood the unspoken. He tried, quite hard, to numb himself with cold. He could cough up things that hurt your eyes, so he reduced himself to a TV Producer.

Luminous Green

I could sit in small convenient
depressions.
A strict diet of gossip TV.
Waiting for my heart rate to slow
to normal
living out a comfortable
zero.
I could finally get my driver's license
at 35,
to travel safe, congested roads.
Or I could create spiralling paths
for all of us,
to spin around in
our orb-shaped world.

I could meditate in the forest for
forty-nine days straight.
Sit solemn & pale as a
phantom.
In hope of attaining enlightenment.
The heart-shaped leaves will be a luminous
green.
Almost laughing as they root into my
hair.
Perhaps I should instead join them in
play?
I wonder if enlightenment is even worth
the wait?

Untouchable Dream

first draft of 'Luminous Green'

I could sit in small convenient
depressions.
A strict diet of gossip TV.
Waiting for my heart rate to slow
to normal.
Living out a comfortable sofa-bound
zero.
I could finally get my driver's license
at 35,
to travel safe roads.
Or create new paths
for all of us
to experience the world.

I am no longer playing an outdated
game.
It was set up to make this generation
fail.
Distrust!
Don't follow their trail of
bread crusts.
Millennials, beware:
don't waste your life
chasing
an untouchable dream.
This is the moment where
the pendulum swings.

The Way of the Yew

Newly formed eye of the Yew
watches you eat your packed lunch.
Can't outstare its unblinking eye—
precious mortality, it reminds.
Conjuring out of you—a ballooning sigh
as you pop the last crusts in your mouth.
The voice of the Yew soars out—

like a bird of prey.
You skid on a banana skin
as you run from the bench.
You feel the unrest of the soil
startling your face.
Then the Yew gives a parting gift—
an empathy in its unmoving eye.

Until the Spider Returns

The forest sung to us
in utopian tones.

The unknown held me still,
in flashes of old memory.

Someone somewhere is sleeping.
Dreaming of the very same forest

that we left behind,
to reach incredible silence.

I'm a light sleeper,
there's a constant creak of fear,

but I don't worry about losing control,
I desire anarchy more than most.

As we approach the field,
I want to touch the soil.

Until the spider returns to the web,
I'm released from conversation.

There are leaves in my hair,
messages in the breeze.

I throw down the animal inside of me,
to create fireworks of dust.

Lying on the earth,
is like hugging underwater.

I hold all versions of myself,
until the spider returns.

Un-homing

A never-ending street took me by the hand.
I couldn't find my way to the forest.
Running from the stench of appropriation.
In the eyes of morning,
I found myself squinting into a dusty pocket mirror.
A startling un-homing.
In the mouth of the morning,
I found my identity fetishized.
At Krumme Lanke, the houses were set to different angles.
I thought I would find home in the forest.
I ended up further into a cabinet of curiosities.
There was hair-like straw spread along the pavement.
Where was it from?
I felt an unknowing of the world itself.
I didn't find the forest.
I was drawn to a silver pool of water
at a yellow house's gate.
A feeling like sea-sickness took over my body.
The puddle was quite opaque.
The wind carried its voice to me.
It hummed: "you don't need a mirror to see yourself".

Forest bathing (3)

I heard trees speaking
to each other in Kiso,
in soft dialect.

GOTHIC

She wants to pickle me & put me in a tiny jar in her frost-white pantry. She wants to romanticize my identity. Enchanted by difference. Expensive jewellery weighs her neck down. Pain cracks—lines behind heavy make-up. I told her—an unpainted face is where it's at.

She told me to stick to topics of the exotic—migration—post-colonialism. That way I could neatly fill in her shallow pockets. To fit into a tiny jar in her frost-white pantry. I screamed: *GOTHIC GOTHIC GOTHIC*.

But—my voice is blocked out by her white-picket fence, and her fading children are howling at the moon again, from middle-class wounds. Her desires weigh on their tiny, sunken shoulders. Blocked out by hot-pink radio playing the same song on repeat. I would rather hear: *GOTHIC GOTHIC GOTHIC.*

I will stick to a head of many faces, a sweet array of sublime, star-splattered skins. Carry on living in a glitter city, not in a town where each over-tweezed face looks the same deadly shade of unfulfilled.

Tenant

Tides rise as I sleep.
I wake up to
a desert mouth and
the sound of drilling.
Panic shooting up spine.
The scaffolding holding the
building together
usually blocks out
the feeble Berlin
February sun.
But a ray reaches
my forehead today.
The warmth says:
Keep it together.
The same words
etched on my tongue.
When you say:
It's a constant battle
against the landlord.
The sky has been
the colour of concrete
for six months.
I listen for the sound of Spanish
rising through the hole
in the floorboards.
Our neighbour below
has not yet been evicted.
I have forgotten what
it's like to feel safe.
Every morning
I feel the walls vibrate
and I breathe in
the dancing mould.
The only thing holding
us intact
is the ethereal thread
between our pasty bodies.

Key-chain dreams

bandaged fingers clutch strange metal
not a red fortune fish curling
in the palm of your hand
not an upgraded smartphone
slick in fingers
but a key-chain dream
code for a badly lit den
where you can't sway wildly to
80s heart ballads
where you can't trust your blinking eyes
to do their job correctly
where you can't wear a faux snakeskin robe
where you can't stay
you must move on
through the dream to another dream
to another piece of metal
in between bloody fingers

At the shore

midnight, at the beach /
the guard of reality /
takes off his tight shirt /

Are you alive?

In the smudge of the bathroom mirror
I ask myself: *are you alive?*
At the end of the party
I turn the stiff tap.
Something about hot running water
is unacknowledged magic.
I splash my face
to face sinking streets.
I will flurry over them to get home
to have something hot in my stomach.

Golden Apple

I circled my slack hand
across the sheen of bark.
Words refusing to walk
straight lines.
Half-sentences,
built on fear,
tentatively reaching your ears.
Unable to get straight to the core.
Your eyes strummed
catkins;
heavy with pollen,
you made small-talk
about hazelnuts
and squirrel tails.
Then as we reached
the apple tree,
We cast aside
inane chatter.
Instead borrowing—
the language of leaves.
The soft breeze,
in slow-motion,
moved the
stiffest branches,
and a golden apple
was revealed.
That's when you
cupped my hands
like they were the
most delicate water.
And silence sliced us open
to the core.

Nonconformity

On a boat from Langkawi to Penang
I sat next to a woman who smiled easily,
she read a novel that was "borderline-erotic"
investigating this other life with curiosity,
another mind's fantasy.
She was exquisite and breathing
lost in the labyrinth of movement—
chasing the sublime.

I drank in her stories—
she spoke of mediocre men
who rubbed against her like hungry cats.
Interpreting her desire in shallow ways,
disclosing their sexual routines,
interrupted often by my hiccupping laugh.
She spoke of the bee stings and brutality
that she had encountered as a child.
Like it was as simple as a sneeze,
she spoke to a stranger honestly.

Apocalypse is the new normal

The living room has vertigo,
all the furniture seems out of place.
We are lit up by a melting
TV screen.
Abject horror (on repeat)
a song of death
interrupting a hearty dinner
of potatoes and meat,
a heavy familiarity
spotlighting our faraway faces
with complication.
Australia was in flames
long before the bushfires.
The irreversible dismissed
by a secure network of power
who say:
Apocalypse is the new normal (on repeat)
because they can't digest
blackness.

There is nothing more subversive than play

the soft voice of play /
breaks the mirrors of the house /
song of surrender /

I am the lake

A flower was blown from mouth to mouth.
Have you ever studied a lake, girl?

You stopped and asked.
Broke the spell of kiss.

I chewed acrid petals: Star of Bethlehem,
torn between my teeth.

You stunned me into silence:
I am not a girl. I *am* the lake.

For a month, I didn't speak.
I arranged bouquets with moist hands.

Smiling only with my fingers.
Now I can open my mouth again.

And even turn up the sides of my lips.
But my voice sounds like water.

afterlife

it came from my eyes
shadowing notes
unsafe
I wore double hands
a burden too clever
a tribute game
pulpy
it came from above
an open dream
afterlife
on my last legs
before

Acknowledgements

'Until the Spider Returns' was first published in the *Between Four Walls* anthology by The Onslaught Press, 'Nonconformity' was first published in *Dying Dahlia Review*, 'Tenant' was first published in *Ink, Sweat & Tears*. 'The Shadow of the Mersey' was first published in *The Nervous Breakdown*, 'Argan' was first published on the Ledbury Poetry Festival website, 'Key Chain Dreams' was first published in *Lucky Pierre Zine*; and 'Sweet Chestnut' was written for an international digital project on domestic violence led by Baris Celiloglu. 'An Un-special Day' was first published in *Anthropocene*, and 'Forest Bathing (2)', 'Un-Homing' and 'Luminous Green' were first published in *Scrittura Magazine*.

I am grateful to my editor Mathew Staunton for his continued support and generosity; Ryan Smith for his technical help with the polaroids, and to Salomeé Lou for kindly introducing us. Thank you to the photographer Zarahlena Froh for the blurb image. Thank you and much love to my family and friends, especially my parents.

Special thanks to Michael Dennerlein—I love you so much.

www.ingramcontent.com/pod-product-compliance
Lightning Source LLC
LaVergne TN
LVHW052349100826
845147LV00012B/792
* 9 7 8 1 9 1 2 1 1 1 8 6 2 *